Margaret Randall, poet, translator, activist, is our conscience, a force of nature, a national treasure who has never faltered in her poetic or humanitarian imagination. She embodies the call of poetry to help wake the world up to itself. Her many worlds in the poetry selected here are by turns tender, passionate, and fierce—and her gleanings from an extraordinary life are more instructive than ever. Time's Language is a salve for these dystopian times, a generous antidote for the turmoil. Every letter counts.

—Anne Waldman, author of *The Iovis Trilogy*

Ever courageous, in these poems *de memoria,* Margaret Randall faces this hour of plague looking back at catastrophes that ravaged Mexico, Cuba and Central America in her younger days. She upholds the "mystery that catches light… but something is lost, fashioned of blood and memory." As witness, writer, mother and revolutionary, she marshals a confidence: "I never doubted / I would do it all." Yet in nightmares she is endlessly looking for a passport before a flight to Cuba. In spite of the closing door of her time, she sees "a future gripped by the music of wings." She is undeterred at 84. A tribute she writes for a friend—that death "doesn't close a door, your name / remains a fierce marker" —describes her own valor and integrity.

—Renny Golden, author of *The Music of Her Rivers*

These poems are like a shield. They become a gentle sailboat plowing the Southern seas as a few fish, algae, moons and stones leap around it—thrown against its timeless journey— its primary nourishment. The sun beyond. An itinerant beating heart, out of violence into poetry.

—Nancy Morejón, National Literature Prize, Cuba 2001

Out of Violence into Poetry by Margaret Randall represents the height of poetry written in any language in the last hundred years and constitutes the broadest, most generous, penetrating and most profound gamble on the part of an extraordinary human being, an extraordinary life and work, on that which we call *future*. This book—concrete, situated, tangible in its truth and commitment, in its fierce and corrosive irony and public kindness and compassion—creates a fresco that is at once compendium and legacy. This is true from the first poem, "Portrait of the Artist as an Old Woman," to the last line of the one that ends the collection, "Promising Trouble When I'm Gone." Here are the most penetrating and powerful metaphors that a book of poetry can give us.... Only a great poet, a poet of Margaret Randall's magnitude, could title her book *Out of Violence into Poetry* and include in it one of the most moving poems I have had the privilege of reading: "I Celebrate." No one who reads or writes will be able to diminish this poetic triumph. As with all great works, no one could have imagined something like it could have been written. And yet it was. Thank you, Margaret Randall.

—Raul Zurita, Chile's National Literature Prize (2000)
and the Pablo Neruda Award (1988)

Reading Margaret Randall's new book, *Out of Violence into Poetry*, affirmed not only my intellectual understanding of it but it was also a deeply emotional experience for me. The literary dynamic of being human is complex, intense, extensive—and seemingly limitless—and at times the human soul-spirit may feel overly challenged. Human expression is as vast as human experience and, in this book not every word, feeling, focus, view is acceptable to all, but that is poetry. I highly recommend reading Randall's poetry.

—Simon J. Ortiz, Acoma poet-writer, Lifetime Achievement Award, Native Writers Circle of the Americas

THIS HONEST LAND

THIS HONEST LAND

MARGARET RANDALL

WingsPress

2024

First Edition
ISBN: 978-1-60940-627-1

E-books:
ISBN: 978-1-60940-628-8

Wings Press
wingspresspublishing@gmail.com

Wings Press books are distributed to the trade by
Independent Publishers Group
www.ipgbook.com

"Your Answer is Your Map" and "Room 5007" were first published in broadsides of the same name by Longhouse Books in Vermont. Several of these poems appeared in *Time's Language II: Poems 2019-2023*, published by Wings Press, 2023. "Waving Goodbye to the Shadow of Myself" was first published in *50 Poets 50 Years*, produced by the Wisdom Body Collective at Naropa University, Boulder, Colorado.

for Barbara

Contents

...we must move against not only those forces which dehumanize us from the outside, but also against those oppressive values which we have been forced to take into ourselves.

—Audre Lorde[1]

Poetry:
forgive me for having helped you understand you are not made of words alone.

—Roque Dalton[2]

Nothing exists except atoms and empty space; everything else is opinion.

—Democritus

---

1 From "Learning from the 60s," a talk Lorde delivered in February 1982 at the Malcolm X weekend at Harvard University.
2 Roque Dalton (1935-1975), El Salvadoran revolutionary and poet. This is the entirety of his poem "Poetic Art 1974" written shortly before his death at the hands of a criminal faction in his own revolutionary organization. The original Spanish reads: "Poesía / Perdóname por haberte ayudado a comprender / que no estás hecha sola de palabras."

Most people look at the world and take it in, they observe it, they maybe try to escape it but they don't actually engage in it much.

Lawyers are not engaging with the world, neither are suited businessmen or arms merchants. Cooks are, gardeners are, carpenters are. The person who is making the shoe is engaging with the world, but the person running the company is not. They are engaging with numbers, which are symbolic representations.

Artists are between both worlds: the symbolic world of people, of the culture they have created, and the other side, the (knock on the table) actual world of rocks and lizards. The language and concepts used to describe the world are not the world. As Bateson put it: 'Don't eat the menu.'

Don was intensely interested in the world of trees and water and less so in the various, arbitrary symbolic systems of culture, especially his own, that of the Midwestern United States. He was interested in different cultures and different ways of making things, but he was not interested in why the stock market goes up or down, or why this jacket is hot this season. It was simply not important to him.

While, for thousands of years, art has been about engaging with this symbolic system—the jewels worn by a noble in a portrait, reinforcing his prestige and power—Don wanted to get rid of it altogether. He didn't want to help portray a noble person or help wash their reputation. He wanted an art that dwelled in the stars and rested with the rocks—a reminder of what is important and lasting, those things we all have and share as experiences.

The semiotic system of culture is temporary and arbitrary, an ephemeral fashion that will and must change. Don was interested in the solid world, in the earth of gardens, in the galaxies, and made art that brought you back to this world, back to where you are, because this is what you really have."

—Flavin Judd[3]

3 Text for exhibition catalogue by Flavin Judd about his father, Donald Judd; Thaddeus Ropac Gallery (Seoul, South Korea: 2023), pp 6-9.

THIS HONEST LAND

Rumbling Toward Eruption

A volcano rumbling toward eruption,
the poem powers to its birth.
Along the way its magma flow
retrieves a secret whispered generations back.
Its searing heat carries traces of women
discarded through the centuries
and small surprises of courage.

A gentle breeze from the south tries
to cool its fury. Genocide
masquerades as righteousness,
throwing obstacles in its way. Lava streams
must choose direction and purpose
as they cleave the land, each offering possibility
or an opportunity missed.

I let them take me where they will.
But no shortcut
can replace those nights
when an idea or silence enters my dreams
or bolts me upright, demanding I rise
from warm blankets and my lover's body
to record a word against the threat of forgetting.

My final challenge is to scramble from its path,
give in to voices resonant in memory
and get out of the way.
This is half tango, half duel
and settles for nothing less than victory
in our dance to the finish.

The Fairytale

In that high mountain world
left after flood and fire
destroyed earth's lowlands,
a mother reads a bedtime story
to her child.

The screaming digital games
of her own youth
were silenced long ago.
A few cherished books survive,
deep comfort now.

The mother reads about an army
of wicked men called presidents.
They lied and cheated until
all power was theirs,
life itself at risk.

They targeted women especially—
the mother shudders
as she reads. But those presidents
didn't count on the power
of our resistance.

The mother smiles as she tucks
a frayed blanket about
her child's sleepy body.
The child squirms in anticipation
of the story's end.

She knows it by heart: All women
unite to achieve survival
even as they mourn their dead.
The story brings joy
but also dread

to the child about to fall asleep,
so the mother,
fearing her child's fear,
reminds her it's just a fairytale
after all.

Prehistory

From this distant perch we claim
our ancestors grunted
at one another.
We display primitive tableaus
in our museums.

That word *primitive*:
a curse upon those
who didn't reach
our sophistication, fit
our expert classification.

But what if they whistled, sighed,
or spoke a language of dance
much as the deaf today?
What if sophistication
did inhabit their throats?

Spiral messages vanishing
through millennia,
earnestness and surprise
undecipherable
by our poor eyes and ears.

Deep in a South African cave
we discover a burial
335,000 years old.

Hand bones hold a tool,
the cave's walls images we call art.

We judge the body pre-human:
small brain,
opposable thumbs
but long slender limbs
for swinging in trees.

We classify according to
established systems,
stages that do not rise
to the exigencies
of who we are.

But who are we? A species
of artists
creating beauty and science,
then destroying it
relentlessly.

Birthing, then killing
what we birth,
defending our superiority
with every
justification.

Did those ancients really grunt and
drag their women by the hair
because no writing remains
from a time
we call prehistory?

Can there be such a thing
as prehistory,
a time before time,
inhabited by those
we do not understand?

Coyote Time

Art is life's only twin.
　　　—Stan Persky

Greatest trickster of them all,
time leads us on,
forever in the same direction,
coercing her best friend, memory,
to help enhance her act.

She teaches us to speak in past
and future tense, leaves
ancient architecture and art
conveniently placed
to bolster her sleight of hand.

Our own mileposts play along:
childhood fears, first kiss,
images reflected back to us
in mirrors we're told
don't lie.

Science may be her partner
in crime, demanding
more than its fair share
of success and barter.
We do her bidding at our peril.

But religion and other forms
of superstition
are worse, lying about the lies
injecting power's control
into the mix.

Every corner of history shaped
by her conceit adds to our
confusion. Even this poem
moves as she instructs
from first line to last.

No clever maneuver can scratch
the itch. At her mercy
and to keep her calm,
we follow her relentless beat
until death do us part.

Their Animal Sensibilities

I watch the newsreel—men on horses
in Mississippi, 1964,
and wonder about the horses.
I know all I need to know about the men.
But did those horses know
who they were charging,
the crimes they helped commit?

Magnificent manes and sweat-coated bodies
glistening in the heat of unequal battle,
the stun of hoofs crushing everything in their path,
deceitful dance of their legs,
and great weight aimed at innocent prey,
even the depth of those millennial eyes
gives no clue.

We think we understand the animals we keep
but know little about those we use and abuse,
imagine they feel as we do
or assume they have no feelings at all.
In their animal sensibilities,
do they resent where we take them
and what we make them do?

The dogs who stormed South African townships
or lay at the feet of Goebbels, Hitler, Hess.
India's sacred cows
crowding traffic on New Delhi's streets.

Elephants nurturing memory, and lions
whose parents roamed the savannah
confined in zoos as we stroll past their stolen lives.

The crow who unzips your backpack, removes
a bar of soap but surely doesn't hoard it
for reasons we can understand.
Whales whose resonant language
we struggle to decipher.
House cats we imagine impervious
with their languid ways and expressions of disdain.

I have seen them all in pictures, on film,
or in the homes of their people,
even those who love them well,
and wonder what they think and feel,
if they know judgment,
have frustrations or regrets,
and if we will ever meet on common ground.

Stitching a Habitat that Can Survive

For Ruth Salvaggio

1

In my dream I walked out into ocean,
no, not into but on:
whitecaps and waves replaced by swamp,
color and texture of oatmeal,
no liquid rising in the disappearing shallows
left by my bewildered feet.

Something big had happened far as I could see.
Everyone knew
and I struggled to catch up
with this idea of a broken world
slogging against my anxious skin.

Far to my left, a single figure walked as I walked,
and as alone.
I called out but my words returned
to dissolve about me,
sinking into a watery surface
resistant to the poem.

When I looked again there were three
and then more,
tiny human specks
almost lost in this arrogant rebuttal
that would not give me back my name.

I tried to still the noise within
and heard them reassuring themselves:
when this is over,
denial dripping from their lips
like milk that has soured,
leaving an aftertaste of shame.

2

I wake but the dream clings to my breast.
Bits of history follow me home.
I clean one nail with another
but suspect the grime is here to stay
despite our privilege of soap and hot water,
rudiments of weather and earnest typography.

The imposters call themselves experts
and we echo their accolades,
say we believe,
invite them to tell us *turn right, stop now, never pass go.*
And we come back for more.

They have imprisoned us in boxes
and we cannot see out.
All the interior walls look the same,
no window punctures the darkness,
no door.

Follow the arrows means
something different today from yesterday
when you wake each morning
after a night of sleep,
even your sheep compliant.

You cannot remember when you heard the first note
of that troubled melody,
ran fingers through strands
of knotted hair
despite such pristine grooming.

When the child reaches for your hand,
asks why you're sad,
you smile bravely and lie.
I'm not, you say, *everything
will be all right.*

3

On desert,
in jungle
or above the tree line,
we busy ourselves
wondering if there is time
to stitch a habitat
that can survive.

Animals and trees raise their hands,
they have something to tell us
but we never bothered to learn their languages,
kept them submissive
to our hope.

In cities with fading memories of space/time,
we try to trick our imaginations
into giving us back easy breath,
harmonious sound.

What to bring with us
is the question on everyone's mind.
What to leave behind is easier,
default doing the heavy lifting
as we swallow the poison.

4

At that moment of balance between night and day,
sun and moon wink at each other across the same sky,
a brief parenthesis when light hasn't yet erased dark,
still waits uneasily for its final cue stage left.
It may be losing its touch or growing forgetful in old age.

It is then we must rely on memory to take us by the hand,
trust its courageous presence in our lives,
listen to its warnings,
breathe its dangerous air.

5

Transition was always there like night welcoming day,
day settling into night,
one season to another
like a mother's love or best friend's loyalty.

Earliest experience taught me to expect
I would always emerge from night's confusion
to a now that would take me in its arms,
speak words I understand.

Once I had a map,
a guidebook,
something I could depend upon
like teal following blue
or orange reaching for red in one direction,
purple in another.

Now we cannot be sure.
The lead actor is ill
and we do not know if the understudy knows her lines.
She may have memorized them all
but what of caution?
What of doubt?

Will I be gone when the future fails to show up?
Will I need to make a choice?
How do we imagine that place where no one lives?

6

Salt is the bitter condiment,
sweat stinging tongue and eyes
that have gathered water's wild imaginary,
used it to cancel dream and destination.

My lungs have lost their hearty rhythm,
invent their own awkward dance
as they struggle to sustain an alphabet
of letters that form words
or even silhouettes of thought.

A cactus needle pierces the tender skin of my breast,
draws dried blood to the surface of need:
desire's evil twin.

Water and thirst kill in equal measure
on deserts where fifty miles away
a storm rips calm,
shouting *no escape* into the snake's burrow
and other underground domains.

7

These are the drawings we made
as children taught to stay within the lines,
early lessons in self-control and fear.

No pure liquid rushes between rock walls
to bathe lost hikers suddenly aware
they balance their final moments
in hands already gone to sun-bleached calcium.

The ancient spring
at the farthest recess of that shallow cave
dresses itself in pale fern,
tells stories of lovers savoring a last shared drink.

Island people are born swimming out the birth canal
to a music of gentle waves,
swallowing seaweed and other herbs,
calling us in a watery key.

Mountain folk wrap themselves in the skins
of generous animals,
whistle through weathered teeth
to a tempo of tumbling ice.

Cities never meant to exist
pulse with the choked breath
of those reduced to a square footage
that has them going to rust.

8

Subterfuge and rattle,
humans morphed to our minimal expression,
neon pounding brain matter
to a consistency of frozen debris.

On the desert we scrape and scratch,
squeeze drops
from succulents whose withered arms
poke places already dead,
battered as they are by spent wind.

There is water but it lives where you least expect,
rain disappearing in sand before it can cool your feet:
not solace but threat.

High above, the peregrine keens its mournful warning,
follows our footsteps far below,
then returns to its rigorous nest.

And we keep walking,
searching as we go,
pretending there is more to this story
than wishful thinking
and perfect preservation.

9

Stop.
Wait.
This is not where I want to be.
Today's pied pipers
would lure us to attack ourselves.
Let us reject the devious rhetoric.
No goodbyes this season.

We commemorate our share of holocausts:
rape of Indian land,
Middle Passage,
Europe's fields of emaciated corpses,
Cambodia's skulls,
the ghosts of Latin America's Disappeared
whispering in our ears.

Rank and file soldiers,
Christmas of 1914,
who laid aside their weapons
to play soccer on the Western Front,
and spontaneous teams
on either side of that southern Wall
attest to our better selves.

The flu epidemic of 1918
was as bad in its time
as AIDS or COVID in ours,
the loss as great,
the grief as intimate and raw.
Our lives and deaths are always ours alone.

Each time we return from horror
to celebrate humanity
there is choice,
a decision we must make
to accept or reject the violence
some call bravado,
others folly.

After forty years and ten days,
the man whose crime was loving justice
walks free on streets he doesn't recognize.
He survived by insisting against the rhetoric
of *us* and *them*.

10

What obeys,
what ups the profit margin
for those who have it all,
brands the questioners disloyal citizens,
rewards them with more fear.
Count me out.

Searching ancestral memory,
I see a safe place to land.

It doesn't look like anywhere
I've heard about
or been,
has yet to take a name.

But it is there,
waiting for us to give it life,
opening its arms to every injured species:
the island dweller,
desert inhabitant,
the one who lives among the highest peaks.

We must go for it,
take a chance.
They say *every future time is better,*
filled with more of who we are
when we inhabit risk
and laugh in the face of doubt.

Perhaps,
but I want to move forward and back simultaneously,
toward a place of healing and memory,
of ancient peoples
and canyons where wind was one with human breath.

11

Despair is their currency,
not ours.
Crowding our screens,
their enticements are guaranteed
to keep us cold and hungry.

We persist,
making our own heat.

Our generosity against their greed,
playfulness against their stench,
their grimacing masks slipping and falling
beneath their own strut and swagger.
Right here,

right now,

we begin to build.

Inhabiting Worlds

We applaud other species
for their learned abilities:
the dog who guides her diabetic owner
through the perils of his day,
the elephant who paints its portrait
or a flower, the cat who nestles beside us
when we're sad.

All activities to gratify our needs,
not theirs. And we claim
they are content
like the southern master said
of his slaves: *We treat them well,*
they rarely complain
and almost never run away.

Given freedom, I wonder what
those animals would do
for themselves, their own desire
and future, how they
might grow
in the context of a world
they owned.

Instead of commanding *fetch* or *sit*
what if we provided a life
to rival Einstein's, encouraged a will

like Rosalind Franklin carved
from the pure humiliation
of her sex?
What if we set them free?

Who would go to war, restrict
their children's knowledge
or experience, invent religious dogma,
spend time on fashion
or indulge in gluttony?
Who would learn another language
or create a government for all?

The farther the species from our intrusion
the greater its range of exploration
and discovery,
inhabiting worlds that wake us
to unimagined possibility.
Take whales in the depths, penguin colonies,
or bees operating in instinctual cooperation.

The octopus might be the best example,
its multiple tentacles each possessing
an independent brain
that can remember,
navigate mazes, use tools
and has been known
to build underwater cities.

This is about consciousness, ours
but mostly theirs.

This is about how we,
in our alpha role, use and use up:
earth, air, water, love, and every other
element we have made a commodity
and destroyed.

For Nina Simone 1933-2003

There are things we cannot name
because no name has arms
to hold their evil.

Events absent from the history books
because their terror
would burn those white pages

and light our bodies in a rage
that doesn't care
where its next meal lives.

Emotions wrapped in dense balls
of poisonous spittle
when least expected

leak from the corners of lips meant
for that deep register
waiting to disappear you

with your impotence, then closes in
on memory: a clinical alchemy
blazing behind your eyes.

An alchemy that finally silenced
the heart beating.
in your wondrous notes

There are stories beneath which
even this poem
cannot breathe.

We closed our eyes against the images
and waited for the waiting
to claim your final breath.

Unkept Promise

I come across her in dreams
or dim recess of memory.
She looks like a younger me
despite millennial distance.

She screams her desire
for words, drawing
accusations she's mad,
a menace to be feared.

She speaks to me of candlelight
and obligation, weighs
intimate need against those chores
abandoning her to yearning.

It's that yearning stops my breath.
I want to fold time, travel back
and give her what I am: teller of stories
ripening in both our hands.

I don't imagine all ancient peoples,
only the single girl who became
a woman fighting shadows
of pestilence and begrudged desire.

Always curious, she juggles questions
that defy decorum, resists
the demand she make herself small,
stay out of the way, defer to power.

Misunderstood, she dreams
a future when freedom
may fill her lungs, lift her feet,
and she will write a story for all.

I want to believe she also reaches
to take my hand, writes
that story for me
from her place of darkness.

More alike than history dare admit,
we meet across this troubled map.
Then she disappears again:
an unkept promise.

A Final Truth

I hold an enormous spatula in hand,
the kind used to ice cakes
but magnified a thousandfold.

I don't wonder how I wield it
so easily or how my hand
has grown to fit its enormous handle.

My movements are dance
as I spread a layer
of old growth forest, stunning rock,

and pristine water across the earth,
taking care to use even strokes,
a bit of patching here and there.

I sing as I sprinkle little islands,
whip sugar peaks
and top it all with a desert mirage

where two figures of indeterminate gender
celebrate their nuptials
in a forever embrace.

I labor to erase every open pit mine,
remove the corporate greed
that swallows earth's bounty.

When fire and flood threaten my work
I used all tricks of the trade,
always coming through to loud applause.

I am a pastry chef after all, adept
at repairing any catastrophe
a grumpy oven or raging storm may bring.

Then I remember this is not my skill,
not my practice of decades
improved in modest increments.

I was impersonating another, someone
who knows what I do not: people
of power or courage and their secret codes.

When I awake from the dream
I don't leap from bed
but lie there pondering a final truth:

The earth is not a cake, I am no baker,
and we are beyond any fix
a coverup of frosting can bestow.

Art is an Invitation

Paint eagerly leaps to canvass,
colors set free
from confining tubes,
sings in perfect harmony
or seeks the viewer's eye.

Like the painting, we are expected
to dance within the picture plane,
ignore observation and memory
where we travel beyond its edges
to summon trouble or grace.

A sculptor's wood may long to return
to forest or sun-bleached drift,
metal remembers the foundry
in grip of paralyzing fear,
disturbing dream.

If you do not bring your daybreak step
and brave questions in anticipation,
a dramatic sunrise will be the tree that falls
in the forest with no one there
to hear its thunder.

We spectators have work to do: emerging
from Petra's Al-Siq, standing on
the narrow balcony before Kiet Seel's
open rooms or in a museum
where Da Vinci and Picasso live.

We might demand more women
or those forgotten geniuses
relegated in any age,
but fail to interrogate the work itself,
its trickster eye.

In stadium or concert hall, music
applauds sharp intake of breath,
silences our auditory labyrinth
as we complete magnificence
in every pulse and phrase.

The actor demands our attention,
the clown expects our laughter
or our tears. Sculptors bid us feel with
our eyes and poets clamor to engage
our breath in passionate discovery.

Like the blind who feel the contours
of a face to understand not only
how it looks but who the person is,
we must cross dangerous borders
in our search for life on earth.

Art is an invitation extended to those
who create and those who don't,
food that nourishes us in times
of war and peace. We fail to respond
and risk a story that doesn't know itself.

This Honest Land

This honest land stretches either side
of a highway that wasn't here
one hundred years ago
and may not exist in a hundred more.

This honest land sometimes appears undressed,
naked in its closeness to pure earth.
Sometimes it wears trees
so voluminous I cannot see its skin.

The crime of war has come to this land:
ravaging its first inhabitants
and committing other crimes.
Still, the rock and sand remember.

On honest land like this, I can touch
its scars, dried blood faintly etched
on rock, lingering ghosts
of children crying in friendly brush.

We won't have to give this place
a new name like the one
on the nightly news,
foreign to those who live there.

Nothing but endurance is demanded of us,
no secret password or recipe
for avoiding disaster when you are
the one who knows the riddle's answer.

Miles and their energy. The ominous sound
of thousands of birds flapping their wings
in unison, translating poems
that bloody us with their truths.

I close my eyes and watch the land disappear
either side of this highway
to somewhere
I have been before, a place

where lies don't stand a chance. On land
as honest as this they disappear
the moment they hit the ground
as if they were never uttered at all.

Place of Dignity

On the tree of human evolution, we resolutely search
for those moments when new branches sprout:
Ardipithecus, Dryopithecus, Neanderthalensis
often called Neanderthals,
and bearing their own indignity.

We *Homo Sapiens* distinguish ourselves by our
upright stance and culture-bearing nature,
although what sort of culture interests us less
than height, shape of skull, or configuration
of bones,

while those who scream intransigent scripture
dismiss the tree altogether, preferring
a fairytale of omnipotent power they call God
who waved a magic wand and we appeared
on the seventh day.

I imagine another tree, its limbs branching off to record
leaps of consciousness, those moments when
we judged all humans deserving of equal rights,
war illegal and impossible, collateral damage
unacceptable.

Homo Sapiens are family members but any other *homo*
an embarrassment to be kept in shame, skin color
ranging from light, the best, to dark, the worst,
and those who rule most brutally
deserving of more.

We might divide ourselves between those who know
that for life to continue we must preserve the earth
and those who fancy themselves exempt from harm,
but that tree's branches would wither
before they grew again.

When respect for each other means
as much as our skeletons,
we may have achieved a level of evolution
worthy of our claim to uniqueness,
place of dignity.

Se murió en el desierto de Nuevo Mexico

For Sandra Stevenson

Se murió en el desierto de Nuevo Mexico,
impossible words that parch
my throat, challenge my translation skill,
demand to know where I stand
in this world gone mad.

In another time they might have been
the name of a song
sung in cheap saloons where people dance
oblivious to the lyrics that move
their feet.

Today they pierce our flesh as we try
to imagine the agony, then give up
and move on, complacent as we are
in a nation where trees are generous
with shade.

Desperate to reach a place where the *Mara*
cannot recruit her children, forced
to trust those who only want the money
she saved and borrowed, swallowing
razor wire and fear,

she embarked on this journey destined
to end in death. Heat as treacherous
as the Mediterranean's bloody waters,

a body with no choice
but to succumb.

Terror, disorientation, and punishing law
come together in the perfect storm
that ends her life, erases a promise of future,
a home that might have been
but never will.

Before her eyes closed for the last time
she glimpses
a watery mirage or remembers
the clear stream at the bottom of the hill
in her beleaguered village.

The Border Patrol doesn't find a woman
dreaming of El Salvador
but the bloated remains of hope
destroyed in a land
of arrogant law and order.

Just one more among tens of thousands
of broken journeys, a statistic
that bores or overwhelms
our smug remove, ambivalent minds,
rage unraveling in shame.

Se murió en el desierto de Nuevo Mexico:
one more piece of evidence
that struggling humans are nothing more
than cheap plastic pieces in the murderer's
game of chess.

Heat

I want to write a poem about heat,
that fearful adversary
now moving in for the kill
but the page resists my words,
its body mute.

My tongue is paste as I reach
for that horizon once
so ripe with hope,
nothing rising to meet my need
but fever and loss.

Sanbao Village in the Xinjiang region
of China was 52.2 degrees Celsius
at 7 on the evening of July 16, 2023.
That's 126 Fahrenheit.
How many died?

Weeks before, Hermosillo, Mexico,
was 121 Fahrenheit for weeks.
Cows fell dead in pastures
as farmers wept
waterless tears.

Greece, Iran, Uruguay, every nation's
obituary whispers on winds
that shear the flesh
from bodies struggling
to breathe.

In this country, we endure records
of our own: Death Valley,
Phoenix, Las Vegas, and Houston.
Smoke from Canadian fires
continues to clog our lungs.

Oceans boil, ice caps melt, crops
wither before they reach
our tables. I try to express myself
but only silence sounds
where a lover once spoke to me.

The news brings color-coded maps:
pale yellow to orange and deep red,
warning us to hydrate, stay safe,
and indoors
where we can escape the truth.

This earth, this place that could
have been our children's legacy
with its familiar seasons
and patient ether,
is burning up.

A future we refuse to contemplate
may read class struggle
between those with cooled homes
and those without,
climate replacing oil and water.

I want to write a poem
about heat and try.
But these words too will go
up in flames as we move past
our point of no return.

Farewell to the Saguaros

Towering saguaros,
desert sentinels
long standing proud
above the agaves,
barrel cacti and creosote bushes
on the Arizona desert
are collapsing from heat.

One hundred ten degrees or more
day after day
has yellowed their flesh
and withered their bodies,
their giant hearts imploding
as they die.

No cooling centers for them,
no rescuers
or emergency paramedics
struggling to save their lives.

I will not compare them
to this heat's human victims,
but imagining a world
without their grace I know
they are the canary in our mine.

The Danger of Reading Scripture as History

Armageddon: last battle between good and evil
preceding a metaphorical Day of Judgment
according to those who read scripture
as history. Or perhaps
just an archaeological site on the plain of Esdraelon
south of present-day Haifa
in the state of Israel.

We scoff at a fairy tale that chains enslaved minds
to dogma designed to stop curiosity
from its beautiful play
yet disregard the Armageddon we construct
with our constant violence,
senseless wars, injustice
and rape of future.

Consider the map. Observe the planes taking off
in that troubled place
carrying death and destruction
to a people
who could have been family
in a compassionate world.
It's only prophecy if we declare it so.

Worst Drought in 1,200 Years

Water only on even days,
don't let your faucet run,
collect rain if you can and xeriscaping's in.
The news anchor's measured voice
says each of us must do our part
before announcing the latest California fire
is ten percent controlled.

Technicolor accompanies that voice,
vivid images and the human-interest story
that hits us where we feel no pain.
Meanwhile, Kyoto comes and goes,
summit follows summit
but nothing is binding
and governments are free to ignore their goals.

We are told the drought that superheats
the US American Southwest
is the worst in at least 1,200 years,
transporting us to those who
abandoned the alcoves at Kiet Seel,
Mesa Verde and Chaco
a millennia ago.

They too faced rising temperatures,
lack of rain, and a thirsty earth
before placing a fallen tree trunk
across the entrance to their home

and vanishing with no forwarding address
or other clue
that points to where they went.

One thousand two hundred years
in a world in which
communal response gave way
to policy designed to kill the many,
save the few, and line the pockets
of those who believe
the calendar will always favor them.

A Revolution in the History of Matter

Life was a revolution
in the history of matter.
—Hans Jonas

We ascribe all manner of fairy tales
to a past where evidence
catches the light in our eyes on hazy nights
and rumbling thunder
battles what we know.

Something resembling a supernova
etched into rock by hands
that followed
the wild imaginations
of elemental minds.

Our imaginations render them
elemental.
We cannot know the energy
required to feed, clothe, shelter,
survive and suffer seasonal want.

Millennia later came a boys' club
called Church.
Its dictatorship of obedience
imposed
on life itself.

Socrates asked questions.
Galileo knew what he saw and trembled.
Hypatia worked in a dangerous light
and envious men
skinned her alive.

It's hard for those who believe themselves
at the center of everything,
and our planet
at the center of the cosmos,
to understand life—

animal, vegetable, and mineral—
as a revolution in the evolution of matter,
the moment that changed the direction
in which we move
and will change it yet again.

Speaking Through the Walls

The oldest among us
remember when
all we had was the postal service:
a slow boat journey
of months from place to place
or days by air
if we had the means.

Earlier there were stagecoaches
often attacked by bandits
hoping to reap
what made it worth the risk.
Telegraph and telephone traveled
cross-country on singing wires,
the sea had ship-to-shore.

On the flanks of Mexico's Copper Canyon
I listened to one reed flute
answer another,
call and response
conversing on mountain breath,
oblivious to that modern innovation
we novices call progress.

A child's first word
in any language
and the last uttered

by a grandmother
who dies with no regrets
are a single conversation
recorded by determined memory.

On our southern border
and across other lines
of cruel demarcation,
messages find ways to defy
the unnatural rules
that profess to keep us separate,
safe.

The internet makes communication
instantaneous in an age
when Mumbai and Buenos Aires
are just around the corner
and political walls
crumble before the power
of any voice.

From Everest's summit
the conqueror
may call to gasp his sad goodbye.
From miles beneath the sea
a voice of discovery
outmaneuvers static
as it describes what it has found.

From your mouth to God's ear
the superstitious plead,

ignoring the magic
of a few perfect words
whispered by one lover
to another
as dawn ushers in another day.

Silence

Silence is not the opposite of noise,
nor the absence of noise
but its own lexicon, a language
that invites you to listen carefully,
parse tempo, tone, bright lights, and shadow,
and then translate it all
in the eye of the storm.

If you are not a dog, you may
miss the highest register.
If your memory is less than elephantine
you don't have a chance
of engaging history. Only blue whales
pursue their vowels and consonants
through the coldest waters.

Don't be deterred by the shape of your ear,
how close your lips are to the desert
in pre-dawn cold, or where your eyes
meet the voices of the universe
transcribed as abstract color,
messages that live for centuries
never reaching their destinations.

Silence is bigger and busier,
it embraces a code no Rosetta Stone reveals,
whispers as it conveys its imaginary history
and deepest secrets.

If you can write and recite it at bedtime
to the one you love,
the poem will come to your rescue every time.

The Boxes

For Greg Smith and Richard Gabriel

*"Any time that you think of is only the relation or
sequence of events, how long a person lives, human
biology, or how many times the earth goes around
the sun (...) Space, also, is nothing. There are things
in it, variously related. If you remove these and the
means of measurement between them, their phenomena,
most importantly light-years, there is nothing."*[4]

In the legacy of an artist long gone
I look at myself
reflected in one hundred aluminum boxes,
each identical in size
but different from the others.

Vast artillery sheds become spaces
where we experience art
in dialogue with its natural surround
and architectural envelope.
Each answer brings its questions.

I walk among and past these boxes,
peer at their internal slabs
in angles contrasting with each other
and with their outer uniformity.
My pulse slows, quickens, slows.

---

4 Note, 1976. *Donald Judd Writings*, 101 Spring Street, New York City
and 104 South Highland Avenue, Marfa, Texas, p. 285.

Through windows inviting light
into these spaces, we look out
at the yellow grasses,
dry earth and vast sky of West Texas desert:
Judd's chosen home.

He died young
but changed the conversation,
leaving us more in tune
with this journey that tells us
who we are.

But now I must ask my words
to keep their distance.
They only create a barrier
that blurs the message,
distorts experience.

The power of light and shadow
wraps itself about me
giving voice to a language
I know without knowing.
I inhabit it now and speak.

That Sweet Place

I want to write about that sweet place,
small and elusive though it is,
brief moment passing almost unobserved
and never calling attention to itself.

Every ominous threat and brutal genocide
elbows its way to the surface of our consciousness,
pushing forward,
claiming space and relevance.

Each devious law restricting our freedoms,
every politician using hate and fear
in his power grab, every famine, gun rampage
or single act of violence.

That moment of pure delight isn't one
to edge its brutish neighbors aside.
It must be coaxed to the front of the line,
urged to claim its place.

Yet that comforting sweetness is what
feeds us, nurtures our love,
promises us a future when memorials
to our dead are long forgotten

and someone is called upon to write
the history of these times,
a story worthy of every sacrifice
made without thought of applause.

Time Took a Little Here, Gave Some There

When we met,
the difference in age
felt like a mother and her child
or a mother and her grandchild.

Then time took a little here,
gave some there,
until we were simply friends,
equals in desire.

Kaleidoscoping relationships
bring life into single focus
until the moment Vietnam
was a war for me, a film for you.

I remember unlocked homes,
confidence in strangers,
tangible honesty.
You live with the fear
that laps our shores,
burns our air
steals identity.

Memory sings out loud
or hums to itself
as the years collapse between us.

Sister, brother, lover friend:
the time of our friendship

may play a minor character's role
or take center stage
with the force of a hurricane
battering the fragile neurons
of colliding minds.

One may die, the other live
without a nod
to older or younger.
Who smoked for forty years?
Who sacrificed for the general good
or was kind to others?

Difference flattens forever
as one continues to grow
or diminish
while the other's story is done.

Together or distant, we survive
in that place we find ourselves
until brought up short by the angle
from which we juggle complacency
or a conscience that challenges
the next fork in the road.

Who We Are and Were

Men go to war, dragging women and children
into their traps of power
and words like *patriot* struggle to stand
among the rubble.

Today it is Putin charging Ukraine
like Kennedy charged Cuba
or Johnson the Dominican Republic and Cambodia,
Nixon Vietnam,

Hitler western Europe and the list stretches back
through history
reading like a primer for man's gluttony
borne by all.

Today, among the news reports of lines breached,
cities lost, refugees fleeing
and updated accounts of wounded and dead,
a small article

warns that Ukraine's national treasures
are threatened by the bombs.
Some claim these are only material items
but I know they hold

the living spirts of those who painted
and wrote, carved and built and handed on
our passion
and magnificence.

Forgetting is the First to Go

Why, we ask, our voices melting in thin air
when we speak of war
or the single orange we cannot buy?
Something happened between tree and mouth,
something that doesn't belong in this story.
We are helpless bystanders now,
alone on a battered map.

When, we insist, did we lose control
of our lives, of life itself,
let go the hand that fed us or the one
we grasped, forgetting
the unbroken chain
we need to feed our own
and others?

Where was the first crime committed, the one
that led so easily to all the others?
What place off limits now
to those who should have known
and those who followed
like sheep on their way to slaughter
because it's always easier not to go it alone?

We look for those we counted on
to record the crime in a book of no return,
eager to accuse and blame in any weather,
shout their names or erase them from all texts

we might read to children
in an uncertain future
when we've forgotten it all.

Forgetting is the first sign,
a plague that quickly goes pandemic
as it circles the globe, sparing no one
in its rampage of erasure.
We forget we are the ones we waited for
whose only task was to show up
and didn't.

Relentless

El mundo patas arriba—
the world upside down.
—Eduardo Galeano.

If I were granted one word
to describe that world
that claims me each night,
it would be *relentless*:
a horde of grotesque figures
suspending me above a chasm
threatening to let me fall.

I try everything: trickery, illusion,
the desperate appeal,
even kindness, but nothing works.
Despite all ruse and machination,
every powerful mentor
or perfect discourse,
I am destined to lose.

Until I understand that losing
is winning
in a world turned upside down
where what we will leave to our children
and grandchildren
is but a hologram
of what the heart knows.

A Nation in Memory

It's hard to accept the unkept promises
especially after so much sacrifice:
those who died and those who lived without,
believing what they gave up
would shape a different world.

A better world,
one not built on inequality.
Rationing meant everyone ate the same,
had access to the same education and housing,
the same care when they were ill.

But when it came to listening to women
as well as men, Blacks as well as those
of lighter skin, subtle shifts protected
the old order, change couldn't be
forced or rushed. Unity first.

Today the young people are leaving.
Old men and women trudge
slowly through tired streets
collecting those rations that once
meant a future of equality.

The dream has become desperate rhetoric
and questioning it a crime.
They still blame the foreign enemy
and they aren't wrong.
But there's more than enough blame to go around.

A nation in memory, like a battered ship
approaching a port
that no longer offers safe harbor.
We want to continue to believe
but cannot doubt what our eyes see, hearts know.

Battle the Censor to his Death

Through 87 years of routine and awe,
moments dressed in sackcloth,
others shimmering,
the one when those black marks
on white paper
suddenly became words
still holds pride of place.

I entered another country and many,
all waiting in books
with pages like doors
my small hands opened,
breath waiting to exhale
mountains and deserts,
taste the salt of distant seas.

People of diverse colors
greeted me
in clothes that didn't look like mine.
Stories touched my child's heart
and those with happy endings
fed a belief
the world was good.

I also remember the first time
a book told me lies
about my own experience
and I learned the written word
was no guarantee of truth.

The discovery
almost broke my heart.

Poems piercing an invisible membrane
to touch a register of genius
repeat themselves
in recitations
that wet my tongue
like the rush
of a welcome waterfall.

It took millennia for reading to spread
from the noble few
to a world of eager minds,
from chiseled stone
and hand lettered parchment
to moveable type
and digital speed.

It's not only quiet osmosis
but how the verb *to read*
travels from page to tongue,
transforming lives,
landing where
I place my hand
on the small of your back.

Today they want to back us
into a corner of shame
with phonics versus
whatever latest reading method
is in vogue, ban iconic texts

because they defy
their ignorant creeds.

They fear most the books
that tell us who we are,
open floodgates that honor difference,
scratch the itch
of our deepest need
and show us the world
big and diverse as it is.

The memory of that moment
when light flooded
my mind's ignorance
and the world's walls crumbled,
has become a cry of rage,
a promise to battle the censor
to his death.

When Violence Needs no Reason

When violence needs no reason
to invade the air we breathe
we may ask a painting or symphony
to take us somewhere safe.

A poem becomes mantra,
repeatable in these dark times.
Some say we are asking too much
of literature and art,

that the products of our creation
are not meant to bear
the burden of our errors
and cannot give us answers.

The time of questions and answers
is long past, I say,
we must use what our minds and hands birth
in this dangerous age.

Some lean on religion,
others on political promise.
Some rant in ever louder decibels
while others cower in place.

I have forgotten how to hope.
Games no longer lure me
into their pretentious webs.
Each day brings untried choices.

I walk among Judd's hundred Boxes
and rise on energy's breath.
Words Vallejo and Rich bequeathed to me alone
take up residence in my flesh.

Our enemies will not relinquish
their assault weapons
or cease to hone their tactics of hate.
War follows war.

When I go down, I want it to be to the strains
of Yo-Yo Ma performing Bach
or the joyous relief of discovering
the perfect ending to my final poem.

What If

Tragedy strikes,
catching its victims mid-step or mid-kiss.
The death Pompei conjures centuries later
repeats itself in current temperature:

fire or flood, raging tornado or tsunami
depending on where you are,
cross-species pandemics attacking
without regard for gender, race, age.

Some claim it is karma, our utter disregard
for earth and its inhabitants.
I want to point out such payback
might more accurately target the perpetrators

but swallow my words.
We are a species of many beliefs,
after all, each real to those who breathe
its unique embrace.

In tragedy's aftermath there is really nothing
to do but console and help rebuild.
The reckoning may be random
but the wakeup call burrows beneath our skin,

keening *what if, what if,*
as we survey a beach of broken bodies
or the charred remains of those who minutes ago
spoke up or turned their backs.

We say we would trade anything
for a few more minutes
with those we love and even those we don't.
Life has a different agenda,

unspools according to a script
we cannot fathom,
trapped as we are by
what if, what if, what if.

What Lies or Truths

I search the *Times* obituaries,
curious and fearful. Looking for friends,
journeying through memories.

Celebrity status determines
if the *Paper of Record* will record your death
and in how many column inches.

There was a time when AIDS, even cancer
couldn't speak its name, and suicide
was written in code.

Today's death notices are more transparent,
attuned to our changing values.
The word euthanasia startles in one.

Women, once sidelined in death
as we are in life, also appear,
although in lesser numbers.

Attributions to authorized sources:
family or spokespeople,
offer up details meant to paint a final picture.

When I die, no obituary will appear in the *Times*
yet I wonder:
What lies or, worse, truths I will leave behind?

Behind These Words

Behind these words live other words:
some so old it's hard to hear them
above such furious wind.
Some have never lost their aim.

Memory introduces powerful words
in public,
gives them a place
where they may take a stand.

There are words that lower their voices
or change the way they dress,
hoping to be more convincing
in gentler registers.

Others arrive in the company
of a drumroll that calls attention
to their boyish charm,
eternal bravado.

There are words that must climb
the shoulders of other words
to be heard, speak softly
but carry courage in their hearts.

Some are called bad by those
who relish punishment
or take offense at their ability
to make a point.

Others borrow their flair
from another language,
entering ours with neither passport nor visa.
No one calls them illegal.

I have banished words from my lips
for spewing hate
or hurting those who deserve the respect
of every sentient being.

My poems search for words
that know journey
is more important than destination.
They grab you where it hurts.

I'm most at home with those
I've known a lifetime,
their worth proven in every company.
I open my mouth and there they are,

telling me all that is required
is to get out of their way,
allow them to show up
and perform what they were meant to do.

The Words We Choose

Between the promise and thing itself
a liminal space contracts and expands,
searching for the air
propelling it from one generation
to the next.

Nothing is static in that space,
fluidity invites us
into its muscular arms,
protects us from the murderous sameness
of this age.

We want to trust that embrace, a music
that echoes in our bones
and the fierce dance that shows
our willingness to journey
without a map.

Trust is a work of art
and we cannot predict its temperature.
Too hot for human bodies to withstand?
Too cold to harbor surprise?

The words we choose to describe where we are
will determine our destination:
a temperate zone
where we will still be asked to choose.

They Made Him Choose

For Christine Eber

He worked for the CIA in Afghanistan,
was loyal to his US brothers
who promised they would take him when they left.

And when they left,
he was one of the lucky ones
who reaped the benefits of the liar's promise.

But they made him choose
a single family to take along,
and he had two.

Two wives,
17 children between them.
He didn't hesitate to pick his favorite.

The woman he left,
widowed in the aftermath of war,
relies on uncles and male cousins for survival.

The woman he brought with him
struggles in this strange place,
unfamiliar words and food her company.

He made his choice
and learns in this land of opportunity
one family is all he gets.

The spoils of war:
defying patriarchal custom
where loyalty dances a drunken jig with fate.

Two Women

For Denise Chávez

Two women, cousins, talk about their childhoods,
strong mothers, fathers with more than one family,
sisters and brothers who have never met.

They say they aren't religious
but tell stories that begin and end on saints' days,
finger old rosaries as if they are Buddhist beads.

Modern women, one an artist
the other retired from a career at Caesar's Palace,
she flashes a smile that hides a multitude of happy sins.

I am wrapped in a warm quilt of female energy,
wave goodbye
delighted life's grand book holds such gifts.

My Breasts, Enchore

Flaccid but far from done,
nostalgic duo
drawing into themselves
secreting memories of breathless hands
and tiny powerful lips
sucking immunization and health
from standup nipples.

It's been a while since they've been
willing to imprison themselves
in a bra, useless to try to tease them
into cleavage now,
those days are gone.
But if breasts could speak
mine would have stories to tell!

Solidarity runs through ducts
where milk once flowed.
They remember adolescent angst
pushing themselves up and out
beneath the sweater set
at a high school dance
or awkward first date.

My breasts know harder stories too
about other women
forced to smother their babies
when hiding from the enemy,

fearing the betrayal
of an infant's cry
might give them all away

and how that impossible choice
belongs to a history
embedded in skin
that separates body parts
too often applauded frivolously
from the pain
of a beating heart.

Sometimes at night I touch mine,
their velvet flesh
grateful for
long years of comradeship
in a world where the female body
must defy convention
to survive.

Each Choice

I wrote my thoughts
until my feelings insisted their way
between the lines,
pushing them to the cliff's edge,
laughing then pulling back.

My words taunted me
even in air so treacherous it laid me open,
exposing quivering arteries of want
to a chorus of mockery.

The challenges appeared in brute disguise,
coaxing me this way and that
with promises of faith and battles
generous as those myths of old.

I followed great men, dragged my art
behind me hoping to win acclaim
in this time and the next,
avoided the whispers

until the words themselves denied me speech
and I listened to their legacy of power:
gentle keening in the night.

I take my language now in easy stride,
comfortable in memory's arms
but alert to each new fork in the road,
each choice.

Not Really Lies

First thought, best thought.
—Allen Ginsberg

Not really lies but alternative scripts
written by the long-gone geniuses
of page or stage.

When you correct me,
say that couldn't have happened
then or ever

I want to create a quiet space,
somewhere I may explain
those other realities.

When I give a story a better end
than the poor one it inherited
am I improving the world?

Maybe not.
But new blood courses through
imagination's lungs,

cleaner air lifts us to a place
of robust health
and hope.

The lie is not truth's opposite
but a country waiting
for the explorers

who will draw its first maps,
build its roads,
write of its virgin beaches.

No Forgetting

Half a century on,
the smile replacing that flash of indelible hate
still screams across your face,
floats behind my eyes.

Vietnam, 1974.
You, a young woman on a pontoon bridge
where the one of wood and stone exploded,
was rebuilt,
then was blasted again.

Me,
a woman daring to visit from the country
that would destroy every bridge
and every home
if you weakened your guard.

Fifteen years before,
in New York a dying man's eyes
locked with mine.
He sometimes reaches out,
demanding I remember.

Or maybe
he only shrugs his shoulders
and I confuse his meaning
despite this film propelled
at 24 frames per second.

He was a vagrant on a sidewalk.
We called them bums back then,
the concept of homelessness
not yet a figure in our speech.

Long before those moments
the angry sneer of ownership
disappeared as quickly as it appeared.
but is back to haunt me now.

When I swallow
it rips the lining of my throat.
You were the popular boy,
captain of the football team,
I the young girl whose every nerve
tried to escape your seductive trap.

An image may live in real time
for less than a breath
yet its echo continues to sound
in body memory.

These moments survive all platitudes,
every admonition
telling us we are grown up now
and must put them behind us,
it's time we are adults.

But there is no forgetting here.

Negotiating Bargains

Desire airbrushed over the face of time
keeps me wanting, needing,
avid for the next experience
to come charging through my hungry veins.

When the paint is thicker,
an impasto of energy rises in my throat
balancing uneasily on cheekbones
proud in their standoff with conformity and greed.

I am not sure
if I invited the artist to dinner
or if I am the one creating this havoc,
negotiating bargains for myself.

One and the other,
blurred in a dance that has me
reaching for harmony
as volume blasts,
then climbs to heights I strain to hear.

Use your words, whispers a voice
from my chatty past,
don't be afraid to tell it like it is
to others and also to yourself.

I still my serious heart and begin.

Trust the Messenger

This morning's sudden freeze
parts June's temperate air
like the prow of a ghost ship
charging the tide
that laps its wooden sides.

Once we depended on seasons,
could trust
the staccato that cleaved our nights
was pyrotechnic celebration,
not bullets of hate.

Today all rules are shredded
by hands
that only care about themselves.
Children alone are left to write
the story of our lives.

Still, this morning's burst
of air brings hope
on the wings of an avian miracle
unknown to ornithologist
or amateur.

Trust the messenger as well
as the message,
the wind and what it carries
on its unsteady shoulders,
marking time.

Memory of Water

Will we remember water
when it has disappeared
and its memory vanishes
because no one can
conjure its bounty?

Impossible to imagine
knowledge long gone,
those who knew
leaving footprints
blurred in sand.

Memory is a web of lines,
a journey beginning
long before we are born
and moving into a future
barely imagined in our eyes.

When we let that future
sicken and die,
destroy what gave it hope,
we lose our history.

Something happened here,
someone heard it,
felt its heat,
touched its hand
and listened to it speak.

They say energy doesn't die,
only changes form
and we want to believe
its new form will feel familiar.

Don't count on it.
If the past is a barometer,
the story we tell
may only reflect an effort
that fell short.

Looking Up

Direction is important to the literal minded
in every culture
who turn their eyes to the sky.
Heaven is no figure of speech to them
but a credible kingdom
with its own relationships and rules.

Cushioned with clouds or paved in gold,
harps and other celestial instruments
sound in glorious harmony.
Some point to a vast place
for all who have earned residency,
while Mormon men reserve personal planets
where they will reunite with earthly brides.

Fundamentalist Muslims promise a lavish reward
for the ultimate sacrifice: 72 virgins
waiting to service those willing martyrs,
eternal obedience around banquet tables
bearing luxury food and drink,
delights of every order
rendering violence heroic.

Christians say these are lies,
ludicrous when compared with the version
they are sure is the one and only story.
Their belief is dogma,
their truth theirs and theirs alone,

the Bible God's Word
and *so the kingdom of heaven*
forever and ever amen.

But the lies are the same
in all these stories
and the devout lift their gaze
spring or fall, sun or storm,
millions of upturned eyes
sure they possess the compass
that signals their righteous path,
science the Devil's trick.

Karma, another certainty for some,
has us coming back again and again
to inhabit lives that reflect
how we lived our last.
Elaborate systems performed
in every tongue and color.

Stories abound
of St. Peter at the Gate
or his equivalent.
Only folktales say anything
about justice as reward:
a land where the poor will live in abundance
and the cruel will be punished without fail.

We might ask these believers
if they think there is no gravitational pull,
if lack of atmosphere
gets in the way of breathing after death,

if space suits are made with holes for wings
or if there's a need
for other paraphernalia.

Neither space station, lunar module,
Hubble telescope nor Mars rover
ever reported sighting heaven
and yet the story
repeats itself through time,
blind belief filling its sails.

Proof comes from golden tablets, holy books
and the mouths of those
followed because they are men in flowing robes
with an authority bequeathed
by patriarchal power.
It's still that kind of world
down here, and up above.

And so, adepts of every creed
continue to look skyward
where stars, planets, and black holes
are oblivious to the fiction
that helps earthlings keep
the followers in line.

Light Blinds and Lifts by Turn

Coming back from the edge of that precipice
to my small corner of safety,
every landscape wears a different color.
All new.
Nothing as it was.

Language sounds in another register,
light blinds and lifts by turn,
even taste and smell
take me by surprise.

Once more I made it through.
Determination led
and my body was willing and able.

But I know a time will come
when the finish line looms
and past victories drag defeat behind them,
relief outwitted by the inevitable:
an arrow piercing my spirit.

An arrow that tells me my time here
is done,
all options exhausted,
every trick impossible to repeat
no matter strength of will.

Every fork in the road will point
in the same direction,
taking my energy with it,
all goodbyes whispered softly to the skies.

I hope I draw my last breath among
sweet memories,
answers to every question,
and that arrow piercing
the bullseye of my fear.

Game of Deadly Wits

Power is a lonely lover,
solitude reaching
to consume each stolen kiss,
every secret betrayed.

The voracious gorge themselves
in gluttony,
then vomit a fruit already rotted
on the tree.

Their speechwriters
no longer offer words of redemption.
They rage and curse,
and people simply look away.

In their dreams they may still
project the grandest image,
cast the longest shadow,
but no one bows before their spell.

Blessed are the meek,
he is said to have proclaimed,
but the meek too
lose in this game of deadly wits.

Only those who take enough
and no more than enough
will cross the finish line,
applause the currency

and solution to our demise,
the prophecy that can wake us:
panacea for this loss
we grieve from birth.

From the Beginning

I might have wanted to be a boy,
possess the significant Y
allowing me to skip over the next questions
and claim my privilege.

But from the beginning
I loved my female self,
saw magic and possibility
where others feared defeat.

I might have continued to follow the rules,
given myself to God,
fashion, cheerleading,
or the boy next door

I might have repeated *sorry, sorry,*
ceding to their demands,
an act that would have afforded me
an illusion of comfort.

I might have stayed home
but instead hoisted home on my back
and crossed every border,
inviting language to nurture memory.

I might have deposited my seed
but instead made of myself
a vessel in which new life develops,
is born and goes its way.

I might have yearned for the power
that extra chromosome confers
but didn't because I know
power exists in relationship to struggle.

Don't Confuse it with Some Apocalyptic Lie

Ominous calm shrouds our days and nights,
misleading in every language,
keeps us paralyzed,
ignorant to action,
unable to hear the canary's warning trill.

But just over that ridge,
beyond the next bend in the road
or on a day after tomorrow
that remains in fictional future,
the weather will change.
Violently.

Two-hundred-mile-an-hour winds
will bring fire and hale simultaneously,
rain will flood our lungs
and ice defeat us
like winter at 29,000 feet.

It won't start slowly,
giving us time to prepare.
The word *wait* will echo lonely in the void.
Its suddenness will scour our veins,
calamity upon calamity.

But don't confuse it with some apocalyptic lie
we might have avoided
by ritual or rules.

We would only have had to practice
kindness, share with those

who need our help,
refuse to go to war,
treat earth with the tenderness
afforded newborns
entering life in wonder,
deserving of that future we've erased.

I Forget

Because millennia of lies have done their work.
Because history got off on the wrong foot.
Because winter came early
and I refused to come in from the cold.

Because I closed my eyes.
Because it felt wrong.
Because something else got in the way.
Because I was afraid.

Because it itches and I can't reach the spot.
Because my memory has turned
to pudding.
Because other memories crowd it out.

Because it was so long ago.
Because it's Monday.
Because of Daylight Savings Time
or Leap Year. Because it hurts.

Because there is no going back
to youth,
and age
has its own delights.

Because you were talking too loud.
Because you never called back.
Because I answered the phone.
Because it rained all day.

Because the fire came within inches of my home.
Because I fell asleep.
Because I was high on fresh air.
Because it felt dangerous.

Because absence comes more often now.
Because I have learned its language.
Because I would never repeat such a thing.
Because I will have to redraw the maps.

Because there is no mirror without distortion.
Because some days the wind
drowns everything out.
Because I couldn't wait.

Because the experts lay claim
and we listen.
Because erasure is nine tenths of the law.
Because I fell asleep and when I woke . . .

Early

I'm always early.
You can clock me by Greenwich Mean
despite the pitfalls of machinery
when measuring time.

Dinner invitations sometimes find me
sitting in my car
or driving around the block
so I don't show up
before my hosts are ready.

This need for the punctual
may trace to childhood rivalry
or perhaps to those David and Goliath
struggles

where late could mean dead
and we had only our wits
against their heavy artillery:
the machine once more,
its soulless deviance.

When the sun crosses the prime meridian
over London's Royal Observatory
we favor our largest star
over astronomical equation.

Still, counting from midnight
or from noon
will always be different exercises.
Context is vital here.

It's not about the early bird
catching the worm
but a promise to myself.

Girl children and women
know in our bones
that showing up is half the battle.
The other half
is knowing who we are.

Modesty

We cover our bodies
without regard
to seasonal temperature,
unwritten code of modesty
changing through time,
called fashion by the smug
and need by those
who can only pull a ragged blanket
about their stooped shoulders.

The wooded path splits,
men and women,
queens of every order,
binary and non-binary
take our cues
from dictates that dissolve
before we get to the finish line,
modesty fighting shame
all the way.

The word *modesty*
trips and stumbles
on its way from my tongue
to the vibrations
keeping my lips busy
in this demanding season.
I wonder where it was born
and how it's traveled through time.

Logic alone
cannot explain its reticence.

Still,
every orifice in my body
clenches before the word:
eyes, ears, mouth, fists, legs,
and especially that secret place,
nameless but precious.

I shield the breasts
that fed my children,
make myself small
but also ready as that word,
at home in a place
only for those invited in.

Asking Too Much

In my ninth decade
I remind myself
to stand up straight,
a daily defense from curvature,

would love my mirror to show freefall
of luxuriant hair
even as the world
sees sparse tufts of white.

Mottled skin, wrinkled and drooping,
pretends elasticity,
the unblemished look
of a twenty-year-old.

I need a mirror
that reveals a deeper truth,
gives back ideas, discipline,
my passionate spirit.

But mine,
like fashion gone berserk,
seems obsessed
with looks alone.

Do I demand too much
when I ask my mirror
to decolonialize
my image,

hold my feet to the fire,
bring me back to basics
and disregard
the façade of age?

Get with the program,
my mirror taunts,
you know I can only reflect
what you are brave enough to bring.

I Can Always Stop

I'm doing it again,
and shame is too strong a word.
It's more like vague discomfort
but only with myself
because I can hide it from others.

My leverage
is telling myself I can always stop,
have done so often,
ignoring the urge to scratch the itch again
and keep on breathing.

It might be keeping one forefinger
on the crack that divides
the leaves of this table while I eat,
counting to ten before my next move

or touching the door jam
as I enter a room,
all those small rituals
designed to prevent disaster
or bring luck,
comforting acts
performed since possession
of reason or memory.

There is the doing
and then there is
the talking about the doing:

one a secret need,
the other evidence of crazy.
I've always known
how to be careful.

After this poem, my tic
is no longer a secret
and I am no longer safe
from ridicule, or worse.
No.
I choose to claim my place
in humanity's imperfect ranks.

Nations

We were young
and had just suffered
our first official massacre.
I really believed those Olympic athletes
would boycott that year's games
in solidarity with our cause.

It pains me
when revolutionary Cuba
maintains diplomatic relations
with countries that slaughter their own
or fails to speak out
against such crimes.

I have trouble
separating humans
from the nations to which we
so proudly pledge our allegiance,
patriotism stuck to the soles of our shoes
like scraps of used toilet paper.

Even here,
where the law
treats corporations like individuals
with all the rights
and none of the obligations,
I'm still shocked when they urge us
to clean our plates,

save water
or otherwise do our part
to make things right.
We are the hapless targets
of armies that march like regimental spiders
across our pummeled bodies
and into our brains.

Until we awake one day
and swap the Emperor's New Clothes
for power's cape,
decide that people,
not corporations or even governments
determine what a nation is.

Cry Freedom

After viewing Richard Attenborough's
"Cry Freedom" about Bantu Steven Biko
and newspaper editor Donald Woods.

Until its escape scene,
the movie was about someone else.
A white journalist
coming to know a Black freedom fighter's truth,
risking his life to tell a story
that had to be told.

The small plane flew over enemy airspace,
made it to safety
and my body froze
as I tasted the metal of fear again
rising in my throat.

Memory is the mirror
where I see comrades long dead
and others whose luck held
as mine did,
perfect segue or piece of a puzzle
filling the synchronicity of time.

Some of us fell without drumroll
or applause
while others grow old
speaking an endangered tongue
few understand today.

I escaped from a country that set its traps
and sharpened its claws
fifty years ago.
Risk breathes hard once more
on tired skin.
I recoil beneath the bully terror
where forgetting was once my loyal accomplice.

Its echo demands
I take its outstretched hand
and I have no choice but to obey,
choked on the bile drowning my lungs.

The freedom fighter and journalist
won their war
even if the first was tortured to death
long before its end
and the second's whiteness
allowed the margin
in which he survived.

Theirs is a different country now,
imperfect but different,
their disparate sacrifices
monuments to a struggle
where justice had the last word.

The country I left with flesh-eating shudder
is still controlled
by the Temple's moneylenders,
laws of avarice,
never interval enough to empower freedom
and heal hunger.

Freezing nights in majestic valleys,
their great kingdoms rising and falling
with the centuries,
their children abandoned
to the smug demands of global give and take.
My sacrifice: humbled, scant, alone.

I search for the words invented to describe
this terror delayed,
artfully shaped to drag it into present tense,
a foretelling in reverse.
Danger lives in my memory
because I know when caught
the perpetrators always destroy such words:
descriptive not of some future act
but of what they've already done.

Watching this film redrew those lines
in my flesh,
refocused risk and reward,
screamed a message loud enough
to be heard through the deafness of age:
you failed, you failed,
and all that is left is loss's quivering nausea,
questions the dead repeat
while I live
with penalty's terrible recall.

Misogyny's Map

Not aberration but brotherhood,
they've always considered us toys
created for their pleasure.

Lifetimes having to fight
for our humanity:
criminal conduct as God's plan.

Rendered invisible,
expendable when too old
or no longer appealing
to their taste.

Too stupid to possess ideas,
too weak to carry any burden
but theirs,

we women nevertheless
keep rebirthing ourselves,
forgiving and forgetting

until one day we will decide
to stop, regroup,
and call enough, enough.

One Last Conversation

A piece of me died
each time a sister or brother
exited by their own hand.
It was that liminal space
I couldn't inhabit,
taking a strand of hair
or graceful curve of throat.

Other deaths bequeathed
some elasticity of breath,
natural forces stepping in
to smooth the borders
of our common map,
telling me it's all right to go on
drawing in and expelling air
through the fingers lacing my mouth.

Perhaps if we could have had
one last conversation,
a place to ask the questions
even if the answers danced
beyond my hungry heart.
Some games aren't meant
to be won or lost.

Our Holidays

May 1st and the *workers of the world unite*
except for those of us belligerent
about Labor Day.

Refusing to honor women on March 8th,
we prefer mother's sales potential
to a holiday that would embrace
the childless.

Christmas and Easter are sacred dates
in a country that still pretends
separation of Church and State.

Each July 4th we celebrate Independence,
send fireworks *bursting in air*
like the bombs they emulate and launch
at every menacing display.

There's Halloween, that ancient harvest ritual
now a night devoted to scaring the young
and rotting their teeth.

Thanksgiving remembers the ambush
of this country's first inhabitants,
a shameful history even when
cranberries and pumpkin pie seduce.

Changing its name to Indigenous Peoples Day
honors resistance rather than attack
but pales alongside the official date.

And recent additions
commemorating Dr. King or Juneteenth
do little to tip the balance.
Our calendar bogs down
in quicksand's memory.

Our holidays are tarnished mirrors
showing us who we have become
in a nation that proudly proclaims
it shelters all.

A Matter of Scale

For Minnie Bruce Pratt,
1946–2023.

Scrubbing or painting over
hastily scrawled graffiti
makes for a clean wall.

Getting rid of words
carved in stone
requires greater effort.

A few days of solitary
won't shatter the prisoner's mind
but relegation to a pit
for twelve long years
births a wound that doesn't heal.

In love and war, as in all things,
it's a matter of scale.
Superficial touch is not the same
as discovering that river
hidden deep beneath the surface.

The superstitious among us
urge everyone to pray in unison,
trust obedience and numbers
to save us from enemy assault.

Despite such diligence of effort,
all guns remain at hair-trigger readiness
and the spoils of war still lure
those who profit from its crime.

Scale and imagination
are savage partners
when we dance to a music
that skims our broken landscape
like stones skipping across the water.

Second Chance

Fantasy always made light
of the serious task,
smiled shyly
when someone slipped her a five
or tried to steal a kiss.

From that time before she knew
she could refuse unwanted touch
or worse
she went with the flow,
winked away the fear.

She learned to stand her ground,
demand respect
from those who think
they have the right to touch
before buying.

Now she knows she cannot
be bought or sold,
recognizes herself in the mirror,
smiles at the sound
of her voice.

Fantasy thinks she may
change her name to Freedom,
her pronouns to they/them/their
and go back to school
to study art.

The Glass

We say the glass is half empty
but clutch a hope
that refuses to stay in bed
this cold November morning.

The ghosts of those who gave their years
to a shining conceit of goodness
circle us now,
a parade without flags.

Our children try to convince us
the glass is half full,
it is what they see,
their bright eyes peering
from beneath tender lids.

Memory may not ever take root
and grow in their young minds.
The lobotomists claim
another battle won.

Chuckling at Funnies

My beloved begins each day
scrolling through favorite newsfeeds,
chuckling at funnies
posted by those
who hope to make us laugh.

This morning there was one
where a sign read:
"please date the bottles"
and another responded:
"I've tried but they only want
to be friends.

Many jokes involve small animals
or slightly skewed retorts.
Most depend on a final element
of surprise.

The value we place on humor
has risen sharply
in these troubled times.
It may crack the rigid armor of stress
but do we expect too much from it?

I admit it is better than counting to ten
before performing any ordinary act
or touching a piece of furniture
before leaving a room:

obsessive habits I've indulged for years,
assuring myself I can stop
whenever I wish:
the addict's well-worn confidence.

My arbitrary quirks smack of crazy,
only keep me calm,
do nothing for others
now that our social obligation
is helping neighbors survive.

My beloved laughs out loud
as she pushes her I-Pad
across the breakfast table.
She believes she is sharing good humor,
inciting relaxation
in a traumatic time.

I love this nod to humor
and also the fearless way she confronts
our darker destinations,
each place we inhabit
on the journey

we recommit to each day,
trading personal will
for funnies,
a moment of ease
for broken expectation.

Following Choice

Time expands and compresses
in keeping with age.
A five-year-old's spyglass
renders memory spotty
when viewed against the crawl of time.

As this moment of uncertainty
rips my calendar to shreds,
leaving some days upright,
kicking others to the curb,
I consider the debris
in bewilderment.

Where can I hide my fear?
How to design
anticipation and dream
in a puzzle I recognize,
a landscape I may look at
open-eyed?

Conditioned as we are to continuity,
changes in pace,
tempo or temperature
leave us choking on our spittle
in the night.

Sit me down in my alphabetical place,
schoolmarm pointer
moving fast in the search
for answers I no longer have,
a collective solution

that allows us to go out,
each in our time,
to weed a garden,
prepare a meal,
sit with family and friends
sharing volleys of battered words:
sentences and soup.

The old expressions no longer work.
They are dried and brittle
or grow a venomous mold
on their undersides,
reach out feebly
in their consent to death.

I know I must invent a new language
but discover my words
are too pale for some,
too forthright or strident for others.

At times such as these
we need a mother's lullaby,
earliest nursery rhyme,
syllables whispered by childhood dolls
or the jargon we toss from one to another

along the softball's arc:
familiar call and response.

Everything feels different,
upends,
wanders in from places
beyond the cardinal points.
Their sounds are carried
on the wings of ominous birds
singing in a mottled key.

I woke this morning with clean air
plentiful in my lungs.
I sat for a moment
on the edge of my bed,
then leapt to a standing position,
my body lithe and strong.

When I opened my mouth,
the words were there,
perfect words
for a simple argument.
I crouched like a leopard,
moved forward with confidence.

My humpback ancestor
guided me great distances.
We made our way
through treacherous waters
as we sang a symphony of readiness,
leaving traces of our breath along the way.

Decision courses through my veins
like liquid fire,
licking the wounds of fear
left at my feet.
It simmers along forbidden pathways
to warm those bodies
that fell in unequal exercise.

This planet,
problem and gift,
rests now in our uneasy arms,
spins in clear sight
as it adjusts to billions of hearts
beating in unison.
Give some,
take some,
as you follow the damage home.

What Grows and Flowers

You might say she sprained a neuron
but it's doubtful rest or exercise
will bring it back.

What fired automatically
hesitates now,
unsure of rhythm or ambition.

No adds for replacement parts,
models with built-in durability.
He says he is trying to determine
what he can do with the ideas
colliding in his brain.

This is a condition
with only one direction,
nowhere to go
but into the ether.

And yet. And yet.
Few bother to look
for what still grows and flowers
in an aging mind.

Tracing the Mystery

I think of you now in wonder:
you early humans
who first put sound to meaning
and invented language
in the remoteness of a distant past.

I think of you with gratitude for those grunts
that became words
and words that became ideas,
our medium for speaking, sending
our stories one generation to the next.

I think of you with love, the brilliance
you shaped from confusion,
the road you carved
through a forest of darkness,
defying isolation, banishing loneliness.

I think of you and wish I had a map
of every syllable, every click,
how language came together to record
a history that resists assault
and multiplies.

You couldn't predict a poet
centuries into the future
would know herself in your debt,
marvel at your art and science,
honor your unknown names

and write a tribute to your invention,
the thousands of different tongues
singing through millennia
of landscapes, temperatures, seasons
of culture and desire.

Translation versus a mythical tower
teases us about the forces
that pull us apart or bring us together,
tells us why questions weigh more than answers
as we trace the mystery.

Sorry for the Poet, Embarrassed for the Poems

On listening to a
troubled poet read.

Two poets of experience read,
their poems are powerful
in different voices.
Grateful and stunned,
our pleasure revels in response.

Then she takes the stage,
unsteady gait
in form-fitting white sheath
and six-inch platform heels,
stares at the audience,
announces: *I'm so scared.*

I want to tell her:
Take a deep breath,
but see this is part of her act,
an effort to turn attention her way
after true poets gave us
their generous work.

She unzips her skin
and expels a knot
of family drama,
says: *I apologize for having to tell you*
my mother committed suicide
in November.

It's late June. The poet takes a glass
of water from a table,
touches her lips to it,
then sets it on the floor.
Straightens, flounces, sighs.

I rage,
then realize I am witnessing psychosis
struggle before us on the stage.
When she's finished,
others clap.
I sit immobile,
sorry for the poet,
embarrassed for the poems.

Signatures

The uneven calump calump
of his artificial leg,
slight drag of titanium
with each forward step
announces his arrival,
tells us he's here.

Smokey scent of patchouli
invades the air
and we know she's come
through the door,
is even now
removing hat and scarf.

The child's excitement
can be heard
before he enters the room.
He comes barging through,
his energy proceeding him
in raucous decibels.

Her silence rages
and all will be well
only when our curiosity
begs to be assuaged
and she tells her story
in an atmosphere
ripe for revenge.

Their signature banging
of bundles and bags
against furniture
foretell their presence,
clumsy or helpful
or both at the same time.

I need no sound or scent
or other atmospheric alteration
to know you are in our home,
only the profound sense
that all is as it should be,
right with my world.

When Fear no Longer Raises its Head

My worn memory sometimes stumbles
on this long march over uneven terrain
or falls asleep in the midst
of authority's demands.

I tell it to take care of this sun-swept land
folded into its forever,
the monsoon rains and whispering wind
that bring new seasons of claret cups to bloom.

My memory and I know we are meant to preserve
the history of those who struggle for justice
in every age,
children who grow and question and resist.

We may ignore the big lies,
tended in gardens of hate,
weeded and watered by those who exploit
the vulnerable and kind.
We may sweep their intrusions from our path.

But we pay special attention to those revelations
erased from official texts,
lost to those who search for themselves
on horizons smudged with maybe.

We keep them fed and clothed,
alive until inclusion sets them free,
violence is ancient history,
and fear no longer raises its treacherous head.

When One Talks, the Other Must Listen

When you can talk to me
about what's hardest for you,
I breathe again.

You tell me talking helps.
True for me too.
But I know when one talks
the other must listen.

Danger and seduction
have become one and the same.
Decision looms.

Survival sometimes comes
in a burst of sunlight
after a storm,
sometimes in pain.

Crises recede,
our bodies arm themselves
for what survival requires
and we move forward.

Nothing surprises
in this old story
that trips over itself
as it tries to outwit memory.

We show up,
and that's what matters
in every life,
age,
season,
identity.

Be Your Best Self

Be *your best self,*
they tell you
without mentioning
those obstacles
they place in your path,
injustices they pass off
as *just the way things are.*

Chin up, head high,
they say,
ignoring the damage
they do your body,
rendering it unable
to stand straight,
walk with confidence
and grace.

Breaking your spirit
is incremental
to the toll they exact
every minute of every day
of every week
and month and year
of your life.

They teach you
men don't cry,
the truism meant
as evidence of power

through control.
If he hides his vulnerability
you will never find the person
you're looking for.

All your life they've told you
a woman must submit
to her man.
Don't let him know
you are smart or capable,
make him believe
the great idea was his.

Be your best self
for women may mean
excelling at pretending
to be your worst,
burying your glory
where it will wither and die,
modeling submission
for daughters to come.

Smile

Does it arrive spontaneously,
unexpected response
to fill a space with joy?

Or is it a mask, mannered rictus
encouraged by polite society
learned and mimicked thoughtlessly?

Let this gesture of genuine delight
claim its small place
in our sorrowing world,

evidence we may still revel
in those moments
that tell us who we are.

Making it Harder to Pronounce Our Names

The longer we live
the faster we move
even when every expert
claims the opposite.

We may look like tortoises
but think like hares
or like cheetahs
who practice speed and cunning
defiantly.

Experience quickens our pulse,
sending our minds
in new directions
and making it harder for others
to pronounce our names.

Biographers might wish
they had caught us
at the beginning
when conjecture is hardier
than memory.

We aren't trying
to prove you wrong,
won't gloat or laugh
at your mistakes.
It's logical, after all.

For what is life if not
a learning curve
bent to the beat
of every working heart?

Where else could we be
but here?
What speed
but this dash
to the finish line?

Poet without Words

I still hear those garbled sounds,
feel my tongue like thick mud
trying to make words.

Translation didn't step in
when I opened my mouth to speak
and the words fell apart.

My ears were working and my mind
but my tongue wouldn't obey
what the brain commanded

and all I heard was thickness,
like glue, or steel wool
scouring the inside of my skull.

I cannot remember what I was trying to say
as my own words fought me and won.
Two or three minutes,

I still hold the mirror of your eyes, love,
searching for meaning in mine,
shared razor edge of fear.

enough for the word *stroke*
to take shape in my head
like a knife dipped in fire.

When the poet goes mute
the universe stops.
I don't know if she was taunting me

for those moments of terror
or whispering in my ear:
Say goodbye to tomorrow.

Waving Goodbye to the Shadow of Myself

Memories and the knowledge they bring
invade the great hall of my brain
as if in the baroque abundance
of a seventeenth century theater.

Those who know the performance by heart
crowd standing-room-only at the back
while the privileged rich
fan their bejeweled bodies
from elegant boxes closest to the stage.

In my altered image,
muscles and tendons
stretch limber as in girlhood,
flawless skin and luxuriant hair
echo a time lost many years before.

My teeth line up, count themselves present
while ears try to trick me
into believing they can decipher
the broken murmur of streams
on a dying horizon.

Time's talent is in its tempo,
slow motion
barely perceptible to the eye.

Hair's silver strands are only highlights
at first, and a wrinkle here or there
claim they can be repaired
with products advertised to restore
that ever-marketable youth.

Muscles promise return
through diligence of effort.

But my mirror takes a stand,
refuses to return the youthful image,
shows instead a tired weathering,
seasons of living with and around
and over and through
all that came my way.

Rusty hinges push back folds
of mottled skin that cracks with age,
my glory no longer a glittering crown.

I gave my fragile finger joints
to keys that spelled words,
my slender waist
to the children I birthed,
my hips to the hours
of sitting and thinking and writing,
feet to walking the circuitous trails
of battle in search of a justice
that would not come.

Bones splinter and break
before hitting bottom.

Angry elbows and knees
want to shift position
but can't.

Voice has lost its resonance
and crows like a high-pitched whistle
in the dark.
Confidence stumbles over itself
dragging blood and heat
behind in this awkward dance
that spars with death.

Still, memories continue to leap,
glowing with dimming light.
Old energy struggles
to keep today's rhythm and breath line,
the power that will stretch this life
I've pushed against every boundary,
planting seeds for future women
who will look in their own mirrors
and wave goodbye
to shadows of themselves.

Room 5007

1.

Eighty-six-year-old female, one kidney
and its half gone,
presents with dehydration,
fever, chills, weakness.
Arrived by ambulance.

When I tell the ambulance crew
they're doing a great job,
one laughs and says: *It'll end
at the hospital door.* Black humor:
familiar and comforting.

This emergency department
does what it can: 1 doctor
for 40 to 50 patients,
broken healthcare system
scrambling to keep up.

It's been corporate for a while
in this *richest country
on earth*, but I seek that glimmer
of humanity through obstacle course
of tubes, hum of confusion.

And the question rises about me
sucking all the air
from this small cubicle. Yet no one

is asking the question,
no power voice claims provenance.

2.

I've been admitted to a room
upstairs, but must wait
for one to become available.
Meaning someone else
must get well, or someone die.

I am the 86-year-old woman
carrying my history
in trembling hands, cared for
by hands from Cameroon,
India, Mexico.

The verdict is Sepsis
caused by E. Coli
shrieking through the rebel
highways and byways
of my blood.

Sudden images of *the other*: Africans,
their vacant eyes unfocussed
beyond the camera's range,
close a breach
no longer alien.

Differences fade as I barter
our shared humanity,
common sameness
of cause and effect,
intertwining of destinies.

3.

Floating from my own orbit
and back, I am conscious
there are billions of orbits,
each anchoring its own
solar spin.

We are not circling our
or any other sun
but black holes in a random cosmos
threatening to suck us
past oblivion.

What we have always known
taunts us now
from behind fingers laced
across expressionless eyes.
Not what they groomed us to expect.

A shift of meaning rethinks
all we've been taught
at schools that bled us dry
for what should be accessible to all:
discovery and choice.

We are reaping the sticky residue
of practices that weighed
excess and avarice, then chose
to bury their guilty heads
in shifting sands.

4.

In this hospital alone, those
of all ages and ills
reach to accept or fight
prognoses that will save
or end their lives.

I imagine the stories unfolding
behind those other doors:
The child whose chance at life
was much too brief, a grandmother
trying to say goodbye.

The charge nurse tells me the doctor
will get to me soon, he's just down
the hall. I think of him leaving one story
and entering another, disparate gambits
in this game of human chess.

Am I the devious Bishop or smart Knight,
the mighty King wearing his mask
of power or Queen
with her hidden agenda?
Am I simply a Pawn in Conquest's path?

Worlds spin out of control
and collide. Humans
caught in corporate cruelty
must wage the contest
to its final move.

5.

I know there is no master hand
manipulating this game
and I know it's not a game.
Histories of health and famine
signal one way, then another.

Infinite worlds spin on axes
anchoring hope
like scattered whisps of cloud.
Mine is so small it is lost
in the blinding array.

And then I am the only one
who exists, all others
fading like extinct languages
spoken by the last lips
able to shape their sounds.

Myself as a random web of molecules
sparring with myself
as the brightest star in a firmament
of brilliant specks: a back and forth
that dizzies time and space.

For this is what I know for sure:
*everything does not
happen for a reason*, no matter
how hard I try to climb the mountain
or give myself to the valley.

6.

The question now: can my
body and will
do what must be done?
Can our generational victories
turn the cogs on this old wheel?

From then on, it's one great dream
dreaming itself.
Doctors and nurses play only
bit parts in this drama
of formulae and lies.

Ancestors I never knew
dance about me.
Children and their children
take my hand. My woman
holds my eyes in hers.

The trick is to release without
letting go, let the gears
engage without worrying
about perfect fit or dissonance,
confident wholeness may come.

It will come, if it does, on wings
of hand-to-hand combat,
carrying the promise it will stay
only as long as the next crisis of confidence,
jubilant gasp of history.

7.

The machine that monitors
my heart, its moving lines
like waves
and blaring numbers
flickers red and green,

is a 21st century Code of Hammurabi
speaking crude poetry.
I remember a friend, one who
truly reads my poems,
saying she found an old one

called *Daughter of Lady Jaguar Shark*
and reread it
sitting on stairs in fading light.
She told me it said
all that needed to be said.

My tribute to the Mayan woman
who brightened her star
accompanying centuries of men
gives me the strength
to banish this intruder from my body.

And I know those digital lines
and numbers on the screen
translate to the words
that run through my body,
fighting for survival.

8.

One day violent winds
bring hesitation,
each song something
I mimic perfectly
in resolute time.

The next, a new energy
pays a call and even
when its visits are brief,
premonition lifts me
on sturdy shoulders.

It could have gone either way
or some other way
still nameless in surprise,
painful or painless
in its gifts.

This time I made it through,
am still here
balanced between options
I could neither manage
nor control.

I might have left myself behind
but rallied instead
and kept moving,
asking questions without answers,
making tradeoffs with future.

9.

I have learned my body has wonders
up its sleeve, stories told
in languages I've never heard
that will hold my hand
in times of need.

My orbit is no greater or smaller
than the next, my life
no more important than that
of the African nurse who takes
the time to smile at me.

What's more: our orbits depend
on one another, performance
larger than the sum of its parts.
I take my place in this scenario,
purpose in one hand, chance in the other.

The eighty-six-year-old woman goes home
to a changed world,
one built of straw and clay
rather than the zeros and ones
of our imposter knowledge.

Surviving or succumbing
is no longer the problem,
but how to use what time is left
to me, how I will bend its meaning
to past, future, now.

There or Here

We would rather be there or here,
on solid ground,
in a place where we know the rules,
can easily choose
obedience or rebel joy.

Nepantla is harder to navigate,
a liminal space
neither known nor foreign
because we fear it
in its menace and denial.

Will we return, empowered
to become once more
who we were: exhausted but also wiser
with that other landscape
clinging to our skin?

This question belongs to illness
and loss, a brutal shift
of the tectonic plates
that balance us in time and place,
a pendulum swinging either way.

Years learning to accommodate
the life we know,
then this sudden journey
putting it all in jeopardy,
Nepantla interrogating quiet.

I practice the art of return,
as I balance love and luck
on my calendar of seasonal change,
this map that carries my footsteps
over a threshold of astonishment.

Eons of Lies

Confused expressions and crooked smiles
greet my stories. I am a broken bridge
fallen into waters
where rapids carry memory
to a distant grave.

To speak of a time when justice
seemed possible
and comrades knew they could die
but spent their passion exuberantly,
I need a new language,

one with different words
where familiar names
stoke bonfires on the horizon
and verbs sing hymns
that ring in your ears forever.

I am not speaking of those struggles
we won but those we lost,
their feats gone to oblivion:
Popé gathering tribes
of different tongues to keep

the conquest at bay for 12 long years,
Highland Scotts after Culloden,
and Latin Americans fighting
an enemy that disappeared
their bodies and then their names.

We search for new words,
a way to transmit
an energy, convey a landscape
unimaginable to those
who come later

because imposter teachers
erase it with the deceit
of official versions,
wipe clean the cost
in every ordinary throat.

Without a poetry that imagines
the why
we cannot conceive
of a future better
than this teetering present.

Without memory's language
we are destined to rot
on a debris field
where eons of lies
will bury us without regret.

Words

If you suddenly realized
you were given
a finite number of words at birth
or before birth in some
imagined waiting room
where embryos lined up
to receive their lifelong quotas,

no extras for those who would
rant their way through life
or for poets.
No cheating or power plays,
everyone getting the same,
accepting for a moment
the lie of some distributor-in-chief,

would you choose yours
more judiciously,
use them more sparingly,
hold back in arguments
you know you cannot win?
No singing in the shower.
No babbling in your sleep.

And what is a word?
Does the same root
with different endings
count as one or more?

If someone cuts you off
in the middle, must you relinquish
the bit that's escaped your lips?

What about words unsteady
in their fleeting lives,
words like *cool, rad, dope,*
or *sick* when it laughs
in the face
of what it always was?
What about *slut* or *cunt?*

Or the same word
in a different language?
I don't believe
there is such a thing,
given culture's power
to hold language
to particular taste and sound.

At 87, I don't know how many
I have left:
years or words.
May I receive a few extra
from friends who fall silent
around me
or doesn't it work that way?

No. Words are ours alone,
like the pain
that accompanies birth,
the stars we count,
your kisses,

or the scent of sun
on a summer day:

not to be bartered,
only used,
seeking new patterns,
configurations
that preserve memory,
deepen understanding,
and make future possible.

Calling My Name

Bombs fall in Gaza. This story
told again and again
invades my sleep with its shrill sounds
and deadly heat.
Ravaged borders disappear
onto a badly patched map.
Origins emerge from the shadows.

Bully power makes no excuse
as it charges a frightened world.
Words like *invasion, genocide,*
and *collateral damage* move soundlessly
on digitized tongues
offering empty explanations, dancing
a fascist jig to the rhythm of my pulse.

In this sheltered space I call home,
I emerge from the warmth
of a perfect bed. The scent of coffee
lures me to a kitchen where breakfast
awaits. Sun floods clean streets.
But the acrid smell of burning flesh
nudges, intrudes, calls my name

in a register I can barely hear
through the din
of false prophecy and accusation,
a detour perfectly placed to

strip compassion of memory,
blindfold reason
and silence every beating heart.

About the Author

Margaret Randall (New York, 1936) is a poet, essayist, oral historian, translator, photographer, and social activist. She lived in Latin America for 23 years (in Mexico, Cuba, and Nicaragua). From 1962 to 1969 she and Mexican poet Sergio Mondragón co-edited *El Corno Emplumado / The Plumed Serpent*, a bilingual literary quarterly that they founded and that published more than 700 writers and visual artists from 35 countries: some of the best work of the sixties. When she came home in 1984, the government ordered her deported because it found some of her writing to be "against the good order and happiness of the United States". With the support of many writers and others, she won her case, and her citizenship was restored in 1989.

Randall's most recent poetry books include *Against Atrocity, Out of Violence Into Poetry* (both from Wings Press), *Stormclouds Like Unkept Promises, Vertigo of Risk,* and *Home* (all from Casa Urraca Press). A second volume of selected poems, *Time's Language II: Poems 2019–2023*, from Wings Press, followed *Time's Language: Poems 1959–2018* as compendiums of the best of her poetry.

Recent nonfiction works include *Che On My Mind* (a feminist poet's meditation on Che Guevara), and *Haydée Santamaría: Cuban Revolutionary, She Led By Transgression* (both published by Duke University Press), *Thinking About Thinking* (essays, from Casa Urraca), and *Artists In My Life* and *Luck* (New Village Press). In 2020 Duke published her memoir, *I Never Left Home: Poet, Feminist, Revolutionary.*

Many of these titles have appeared in Spanish translation from Siglo XXI, Alforja, Ediciones de Medianoche, and Heredad in Mexico; Casa de las Américas, Ediciones Matanzas, and Vigía in Cuba; Abisinia and Tinta Limón in Argentina, Rumbo in Uruguay, and small independent publishers in Nicaragua, Brazil, Ecuador, Peru, Colombia, Venezuela, Spain, Holland, Japan, Turkey, and India.

Margaret also translates from the Spanish. She has produced poetry collections by Roberto Fernández Retamar, Roque Dalton, Otto-René Castillo, Carlos María Gutiérrez, Daisy Zamora, Kelly Martínez, Israel Domínguez, Alfredo Zaldívar, Laura Ruíz, Chely Lima, Rita Valdivia, Reynaldo García Blanco, Yanira Marimón, and Gaudencio Rodríguez Santana, among others; novels by Freddy Prestol Castillo, Juan Antonio Hernández, and Tomás Modesto Galán; memoirs by Gregory Randall, Lurgio Gavilán Sánchez, and Stefano Varese; and anthologies of Cuban poetry and short stories, Ecuadorean poetry, US poets for Mexico, and Beat Poets in Spanish. She has read her own work and delivered keynote addresses in hundreds of venues throughout the United States, Latin America, and other countries.

Two of Randall's photographs are in the Capitol Art Collection in Santa Fe. In 1960 Randall was a recipient of a Carnegie Fund for Writers Aid Grant and a grant from the American Academy of Arts and Letters revolving fund for writers in need. In 1989 she was a co-winner of the Mencken Award, and in 1990 she received a Lillian Hellman and Dashiell Hammett grant for writers victimized by political repression. The Barbara Deming Money for Women Award was given to her in 1997, and in 2004 she received the PEN New Mexico Dorothy Doyle Lifetime Achievement Award for Writing and Human

Rights Activism. Randall was awarded the 2017 *Medalla al Mérito Literario* from *Literatura en el Bravo*, Ciudad Juárez, Mexico. In 2018 she was awarded the "Poet of Two Hemispheres" prize by *Poesía en Paralelo Cero* in Quito, Ecuador. In 2019 she earned an honorary doctorate of letters from the University of New Mexico. In 2020 she received the George Garrett Award from the Association of Writers & Writing Programs (AWP) and the Paulo Freire Award from Chapman University. In 2022 she won the City of Albuquerque's Creative Bravo Award. Randall lives in Albuquerque with her partner (now wife) of more than 37 years, the painter Barbara Byers, and travels extensively to read, lecture and teach.

Colophon

This first edition of *This Honest Land* by
Margaret Randall, has been printed on 60
pound "natural" paper containing a percent-
age of recycled fiber. Book titles have been set
in Charlemagne Standard type, poem titles
and text in Adobe Caslon type. All Wings
Press books, 1995 to 2024, were designed
by Bryce Milligan.

Wings Press titles are distributed to the trade by the
Independent Publishers Group
www.ipgbook.com
and in Europe by Gazelle
www.gazellebookservices.co.uk

Also available as an ebook.